GREAT STORIES *from the* OLD TESTAMENT

tales from the Old Testament
retold for children

Great Stories from the Old Testament
© 2023 North Parade Publishing,
Written by Janice Emmerson
Illustrations by QBS Learning

Published by North Parade Publishing, Bath BA1 1LF, United Kingdom

All rights are reserved. No part of this publication may be reproduced, stored in a retrieval system or transmitted in any form or by any means, electronic, mechanical, photocopying, recording or otherwise, without the prior permission of the Publisher

Printed in China

Contents

The Stolen Blessing
Genesis 25–27
4

Tricked
Genesis 29
6

Joseph, the Dreamer
Genesis 37–47
8

Three Hundred Men
Judges 7
12

A Loyal Daughter-in-Law
Ruth 1–4
14

Elijah, the Prophet
1 Kings 17–18
16

A Double Dose of Spirit
2 Kings 2
20

Washed Clean
2 Kings 5
22

The Potter and His Clay
Jeremiah 18, 29; 2 Kings 25
24

Rebuilding Jerusalem
Nehemiah 1–4, 8
26

Jonah and the Very Big Fish
Jonah 1–3
29

The Stolen Blessing

Jacob was Abraham's grandson. His father was Isaac, and his mother was Rebecca. He had a twin brother, Esau, born just before Jacob. But because he had been born first, he was going to inherit his father's role as head of the family. His share of the inheritance would be twice as large as Jacob's. And his father's blessing would go to him.

But Esau lost his rights as the firstborn son. In fact, he gave them away. And this is how it happened.

One day, Esau returned famished after a long day out hunting. Jacob was busy making a delicious stew, but would only let him have some if Esau agreed to give him his rights as the firstborn son. Esau was so hungry and the stew smelt so good that he actually agreed!

Some time after that, Jacob managed to cheat his brother out of his father's blessing, too. By now, Isaac was very old, and almost completely blind. One day he called to Esau to go hunting and make him a meal of his favourite meat. "Then I will give you my blessing," he promised. And off Esau went.

But Rebecca wanted the blessing to go to her favourite son. She made Jacob fetch two young goats, prepared a dish from them, and told Jacob to take it to his father. But before he went, she used the goat skins to cover his arms and neck—for Esau was very hairy!

Isaac thought his son sounded a bit different. "Come close," he said. "Let me feel you." When Jacob came to his bedside, Isaac touched his son's skin. "You sound like Jacob," he muttered, confused, "but you feel like Esau." So he gave Jacob his blessing.

When Esau found out, he was furious! Rebecca sent Jacob to stay with his uncle, to keep him safe from his brother's vengeance. But the blessing had been given, and could not be taken back. Jacob would rule over his brother!

Tricked

Jacob spent rather a lot of time with his uncle Laban, for soon after arriving, he fell head over heels in love with Laban's youngest daughter, Rachel. Cunning Laban promised his nephew that if he would work for him for a short period—seven years should do it—he could take Rachel as his bride at the end of that time.

As far as Jacob was concerned, seven years was a small price to pay if he could wed his beloved Rachel afterwards.

The seven years flew by, and after they were over Laban held a huge party and brought his daughter to Jacob to marry. They spent the night together and when Jacob woke up, he was shocked and dismayed to find lying beside him, not Rachel, but her elder sister Leah (she had been wearing a heavy veil the night before)! Laban had tricked him.

Jacob was furious, but Laban stood his ground. "Around here, the younger daughter can't marry before an older daughter. But I'll tell you what—see out the wedding ceremony. That's just one week. And at the end of that time you can take Rachel as your wife, too." (In those days men often had more than one wife.) "You'll have to work for me for another seven years, of course. I can't be fairer than that!"

Jacob was seething, but what could he do? He loved Rachel with all his heart, and so everything happened just as Laban had wanted.

But what about poor Leah? It was Rachel that Jacob loved, and Leah knew that she was only there on sufferance. But God took pity on her. Jacob might not have loved Leah, but God did, and he sent her many sons and one daughter to console her and look after her. It would be many years before Rachel would have a child.

Joseph, the Dreamer

Joseph was Jacob's favourite son. Jacob had twelve sons, but he loved none of them as much as he loved Joseph, for his mother was Rachel. To show Joseph how much he meant to him, Jacob bought him a wonderful coat, far finer than anything his brothers had to wear.

Now, Joseph's brothers were—not surprisingly—rather put out by this. But they grew even angrier when Joseph told them about the strange dreams he had had—dreams which seemed to say that one day he would be far greater than his brothers, and even than his parents!

The jealous brothers were so mad that they decided to be rid of their irritating brother. They planned to kill him, but then they realised that they could earn some money by selling him as a slave. They told their father that their brother had been taken by a wild animal—poor Jacob wept.

Meanwhile, the slave traders took Joseph to Egypt, where he worked for a

rich man. Due to a misunderstanding, he ended up in prison where he met two men—Pharoah's baker and Pharoah's steward.

These two men had strange dreams, and Joseph was able to explain to them what they meant. Pharoah forgave the steward, and he went back to work for him, but the baker was executed.

Some time later, when Pharoah had strange dreams himself, the steward remembered Joseph, and he was sent for to explain the dreams. Joseph told Pharoah that his dreams meant that Egypt was to be blessed with seven years of good crops, but that they would be followed by seven years of famine.

Pharaoh was so impressed with Joseph that he put him in charge of planning for the famine. Now he was second only to Pharaoh himself! When the bumper harvests that he had forecast came to pass, he made sure that all the farmers put some of the crops aside, and these were gathered up and safely stored in enormous storehouses. So when the dreadful years of famine came, the Egyptians were well prepared.

But beyond Egypt it was a different story. People everywhere began to starve. In Canaan Joseph's brothers were among those who had no food. Jacob decided to send his sons to Egypt to see if they could buy some grain.

The brothers travelled to Egypt and begged Joseph for some food—not one of them recognized him in his fine clothes! Joseph decided to test them. He gave them sacks of grain, but secretly planted a silver cup in the sack of the youngest brother, Benjamin, before the brothers set off, across the desert.

The unsuspecting brothers were horrified when soldiers came after them and tore open the sacks—and out tumbled the silver cup! They were dragged before Joseph, and they pleaded for his forgiveness.
They told him God was punishing them for their wickedness long ago. Joseph said he would set them all free—all apart from Benjamin!

The brothers wept, and begged Joseph to take one of them instead, for they knew it would break their father's heart to lose Benjamin after losing Joseph. Now Joseph knew that they had really changed.

"Can't you see that it's me?" he cried. "Joseph?" and he hugged his brothers. "Don't worry about the past!" he said. "It was all God's plan. He sent me here so I could save you!"

Pharaoh told Joseph to bring his father and his brothers' families to Egypt, where he would give them the finest land to farm. So Jacob was at last reunited with his beloved son!

Three Hundred Men

The people had turned away from God, and now a new enemy threatened them. For seven years the Hebrews had been terrorized by the Midianites. They called out to God, "Help us!" they begged.

God sent them a new hero, Gideon. He gathered a large army, but God told him he had too many men, and to send any home who were scared. After that he only had ten thousand men left.

"Still too many," said God. "Tell them to go and drink from the river. Take only those who cup the water in their hands."

Now only three hundred men were left! How on earth could they defeat the Midianites? There were over a hundred thousand of them! But God reassured Gideon, "With these three hundred men I will deliver the Midianites into your hands."

Gideon trusted in God, but still, that night as he looked down upon the endless tents of his enemy, he couldn't but help feel anxious. God told Gideon to creep down to the enemy camp and listen to what they were saying, and when he heard them talking about their dreams, he realised how terrified the Midianites were of him and his army!

By the time Gideon returned to his own tent he was feeling reassured. He called to his men to get up and divided them into three groups. He gave each man a trumpet and a jar with a torch in it, then gave them some very specific instructions.

In no time at all Gideon's men had surrounded the camp. Then, at a signal from Gideon, they all blew their trumpets and shouted out loudly, and smashed their jars on the ground.

The sudden noise and light scared the Midianites out of their wits. They had no idea what was going on, and in the panic began turning on one another, before fleeing in terror.

This was how Gideon and God defeated the Midianites with just three hundred men.

A Loyal Daughter-in-Law

"I'm staying with you, and that's that!" Ruth said kindly but firmly.

Naomi had decided that it was time to head back to her home town of Bethlehem. Her husband and her sons had died, and she was all alone in the world apart from her two daughters-in-law. She told them to stay behind, for she knew that her life in Bethlehem would be hard. Orpah reluctantly said good-bye and went home to her family. But Ruth would not leave her.

"You shouldn't come with me," begged Naomi. "I have nothing to give you—my life will be hard."

"Please don't make me leave you!" cried Ruth. "Let me go with you! Wherever you go, I will go. Your people will be my people. Your God will be my God. Don't ask me to go!"

So it was that Ruth and Naomi travelled to Bethlehem. Life was difficult, just as Naomi had warned. But Ruth was not easily disheartened. It was harvest time, and she decided to go into the fields where the people were working. "Maybe they will let me gather some of the grain that they drop," she said to Naomi hopefully.

The field belonged to a rich man named Boaz. When he saw Ruth in the fields he told his workers to share their food with her and to be kind to her. And he told her she would always be welcome in his fields, for he had heard about her loyalty to Naomi.

Boaz was related to Naomi. When Ruth returned home with a basket full of grain and told her mother-in-law what had happened, Naomi knew that God was looking after them. And look after them he did, for in time Boaz married Ruth, and they had a beautiful baby boy, and Naomi became a proud and devoted grandmother.

Do you know what the name Naomi means? It means happy—and for the first time in a long while, that's exactly what Naomi was!

Elijah, the Prophet

Elijah was one of God's prophets. Israel had split in two—in the south the tribes of Judah and Benjamin were loyal to King Solomon's son, but the ten northern tribes broke away. Wicked King Ahab was the ruler of the northern kingdom, and he allowed the worship of the false god, Baal. Elijah tried his best to bring the people back to God.

God sent a drought throughout the land. Elijah warned the king that for the next few years there would be neither rain nor dew throughout the land. Needless to say, Ahab wasn't too thrilled with this news. And he wasn't pleased with Elijah.

God sent Elijah away to a safe place, where ravens brought him food every morning and evening, and he drank from a small brook.

When the brook dried up, God sent Elijah to Sidon. At the city gates Elijah spotted a poor widow collecting sticks. He asked for some water, and she turned to fetch some, but when he asked her for some bread, too, she told him sadly that she only had enough flour and oil for one last loaf for her and her son.

Elijah said soothingly, "Don't worry. Make a small loaf of bread for me, and then make some for you and your son. God has promised that the flour and the oil won't run out before the drought ends!"

The widow did as the prophet had asked, and was amazed to find that when she had made the loaves of bread there was still flour and oil left over. And so it went on, for every day when she made bread there was still enough flour and oil to make another loaf!

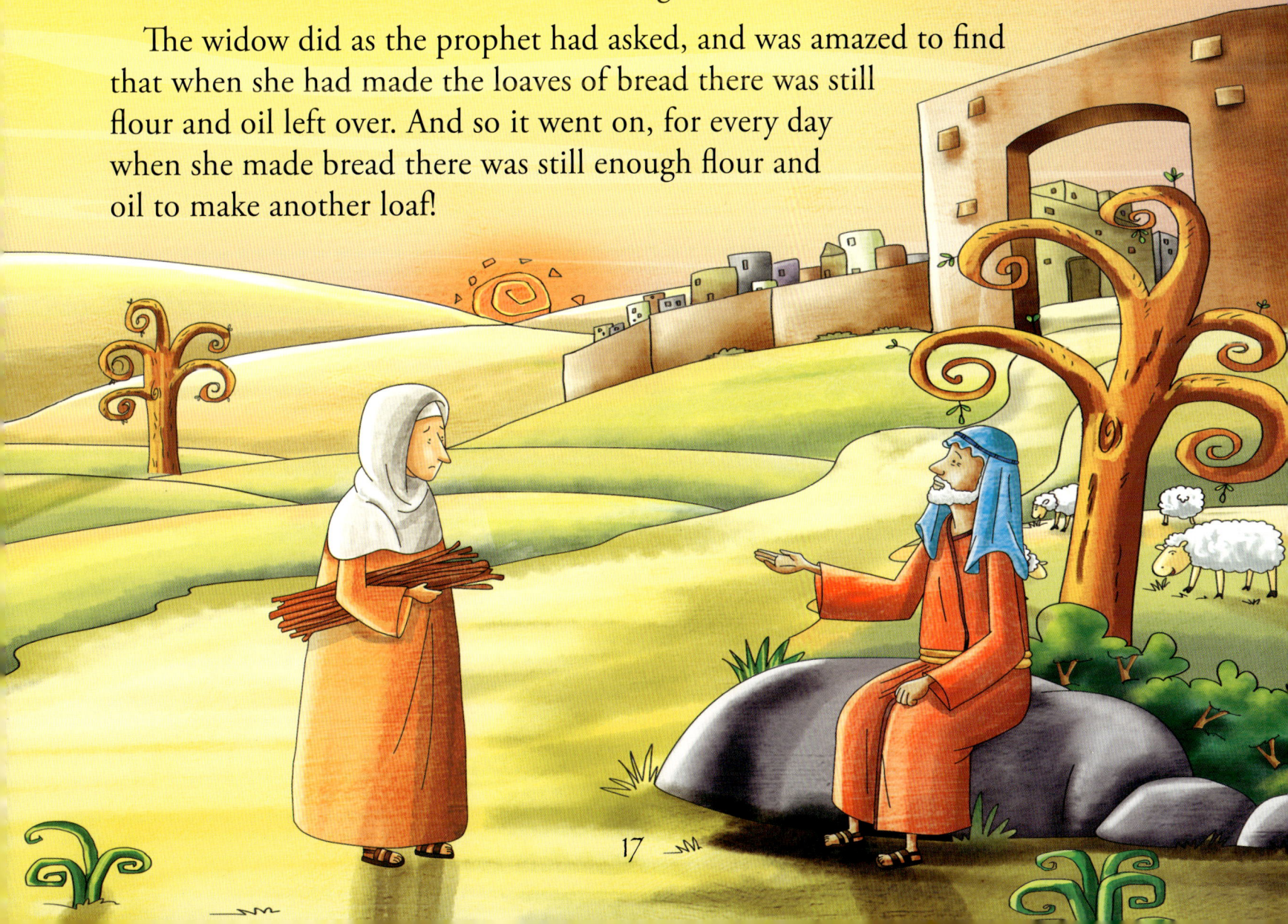

But although the widow and her son did not go hungry, the little boy fell ill—desperately ill—and all too soon he stopped breathing!

The widow was distraught. "Why did you come here?" she said to Elijah despairingly. "Did you come to punish me by killing my son?"

Elijah replied calmly, "Give me your son," and he carried the boy to the room upstairs that he was using, and placed him gently on his bed. Then he cried out to God, "Oh Lord, why have you brought such a tragedy upon this woman? She has been so good to me!"

He stretched out upon the boy three times, and called to God, and begged him to bring him back to life. God heard Elijah's prayer, and the boy began to breathe. Elijah carried him downstairs to his mother, who wept tears of joy when she saw that her beloved son was alive.

"You truly are a man of God!" she said in awe.

After three years Elijah told King Ahab to gather the people of Israel and the prophets of Baal at Mount Carmel. It was time for them to learn who was the true God of Israel.

He told the prophets of Baal to prepare a bull for sacrifice, and to call to their god to start the fire. The prophets prepared the sacrifice, and called to Baal to help them. They prayed and they tore their clothes and danced wildly and cried out. But nothing happened!

"Enough," said Elijah at last. "Now it's my turn." Then he prepared the sacrifice—even telling those around him to pour water on top of everything—and called upon God to show his true power.

And at that very moment fire came down from God and burned up the sacrifice, the wood, the stones, and even the water in the ditch!

The people fell to their knees. "It's true!" they cried. "The Lord is God!"

A Double Dose of Spirit

Elisha was Elijah's pupil. One day, when Elijah was very old, he was walking by the river Jordan with Elisha, and asked him if there was anything he wanted to request before he left. Elisha replied gravely, "Master, I should like to inherit your spirit—double your spirit!—so that I can continue your work when you are gone."

Right then a chariot of fire descended from heaven, drawn by horses of fire! Elijah was taken up to heaven in a whirlwind.

When the skies calmed, Elisha saw Elijah's cloak on the ground. With a heart full of wonder and awe, he took the cloak and walked to the bank of the river. He hit the river with the cloak and the waters parted before him and he crossed over.

When the other prophets saw, they understood that Elijah's spirit had passed to Elisha, and they bowed before him in respect.

One day a woman came to see Elisha to beg for his help. Her husband had died and left her in debt, and the man she owed had threatened to take her two sons as slaves in repayment!

Now, Elisha had no money to give her, but he thought carefully, and then he asked her what she had at home. "Nothing but a small jar of olive oil!" replied the woman despondently.

Elisha told her to go to her neighbours and ask if she could borrow any empty jars. "Find as many as you can!" he urged, "then go home with your sons and shut all the doors. Then pour the oil into the jars."

The woman did as he said. She and her sons gathered lots of jars, then shut themselves inside. She poured the oil into a jar. As soon as it was full, she filled another, and then another. She poured and poured until there were no more jars left. When she looked in the small jar she saw it was finally empty!

She and her sons were able to sell the jars of oil and repay their debt.

There was even money left over for them to live on!

Washed Clean

Naaman might well have been a commander of the army of Syria, but he was feeling decidedly miserable, for he had a terrible skin disease. One of his slaves was a young Israelite girl. She suggested that her master should travel to see the wonderful prophet Elisha, who lived in Samaria in Israel.

But when Naaman arrived at Elisha's house, he was rather disgruntled when the prophet sent his servant out. He probably expected the prophet to come out himself and bow before him!

Instead, the servant gave him a message. "Go and wash in the Jordan River. Bathe in it seven times and your skin will be healed, and you will be clean."

Naaman was furious. "Elisha can't be bothered to come and heal me himself!" he sulked. "If he thinks I'm going to go and bathe in that filthy river just because he says so then he can think again!"

He was on the point of storming off in disgust when his servant managed to persuade him that he might as well give it a try.

So Naaman swallowed his pride and went down to the river and dipped himself in it seven times. And guess what? When he emerged after the seventh time all the sores had completely disappeared and his skin was soft and smooth and healthy.

He rushed to thank Elisha. He stood before the prophet and bowed his head. "Now I know that yours is the one true God!" he said humbly.

The Potter and His Clay

The years passed, and Judah and Jerusalem turned further and further from God. He sent another prophet, Jeremiah, to warn them.

One day, Jeremiah sat in a potter's workshop, watching him work. The potter took pieces of rough clay, then skillfully and lovingly shaped them into beautiful vases and useful plates and bowls. Sometimes the clay didn't do what the potter wanted it to. Then he would start again and make it into something different.

"Israel is like the clay," God told Jeremiah. "I am trying to mould something special out of it. But if it doesn't work out, I'm prepared to start from scratch. If Israel becomes evil, I will change what I had planned for it, but if it repents I will give it another chance."

Jeremiah tried to warn the people, but they just threw him in jail!

The people had refused to listen to God's warnings. They had been given their final chance, and so Jerusalem fell to a new enemy—Babylon, and its mighty ruler, Nebuchadnezzar. All the strong, skilled people from the city were taken away to Babylon to work. Those who were left behind thanked their lucky stars, but actually they were in a worse position, for they hadn't learned the error of their ways.

The new king began to think that he was powerful enough to stand up to Babylon. Jeremiah tried to warn him, but the king would not listen. And as night follows day, Babylon once again bore down on the city of Jerusalem and this time they burned the city to the ground.

God had punished his children, but he had not stopped loving them. He knew they needed this hard lesson— to be reshaped, like the potter's clay—and that they would learn from it. They would return to his arms, and one day would come home, with God by their side.

Rebuilding Jerusalem

Jerusalem had been conquered by the Babylonian forces. For years the Jews had been exiled from their homeland, slaves to their enemies. But at long last the new ruler of the empire allowed the exiles to return home. While filled with gladness, they returned to a ruined city. At last the temple was rebuilt, but the walls remained in ruins.

Far away in Babylonia, an exile named Nehemiah worked for Emperor Araxerxes. He asked if he might go back and help his people, and Araxerxes gave him permission. But when he arrived in Jerusalem, Nehemiah was shocked at how bad things were. Hardly any of the wall was still standing!

The next morning he gathered together the leaders of the people and spoke to them sternly. "You should be ashamed of yourselves!" he declared. "We need to rebuild the walls and make new gates. And we need to do it now!"

Nehemiah's coming filled the people with new energy. Everyone helped out with the building work.

But the Samaritans were far from pleased. They didn't want Jerusalem to be strong and safe behind big, sturdy walls. So they tried to discourage their neighbours, but the Jews just put their heads down and ignored the taunts. They had more important things to do than listen to insults.

The Samaritans had tried to discourage the Jews by teasing them. When that didn't work, they threatened them. But Nehemiah knew that God wanted them to plough ahead, and he knew God would look after them. He told every man to carry weapons, and he divided them into groups—one group would work while the other stood guard.

Every day they began work at the crack of dawn, and they were still working when the stars appeared in the night sky.

They worked, and worked … and in fifty-two days the walls were finished and Jerusalem was protected!

Jonah and the Very Big Fish

God had told Jonah to go to Nineveh to give an important message to the people there. He wanted him to tell them to stop doing all the bad things that they were doing.

But Jonah didn't want to go, because he guessed that God would forgive the people of Ninevah if they repented, and he didn't like them. So instead he got on a ship heading in the wrong direction—about two and a half thousand miles in the wrong direction!

But you really can't run away from God. It doesn't matter how far you go, he'll still be there. And Jonah should have known that.

He fell fast asleep on the ship. A dreadful storm blew up. The ship rolled in the frothy waters, and waves slammed over the sides. The sailors were panic-stricken. "Someone must have angered one of the gods!" they wailed (they weren't Jews). "We're all going to die!"

Jonah knew in his heart that God had sent this storm because of him. "It's my fault," he owned up above the roar of the waves. "I tried to run away from God and he is angry with me. You should throw me overboard, and then the rest of you will be safe!"

Deep inside the belly of the fish everything was dark (and probably rather smelly given all the rotten seaweed and fishbones around!) But Jonah was alive.

For three days and three nights Jonah sat inside the fish. He had plenty of time to think about what he had done, and to realise how silly he had been.

After three days the fish spat Jonah safely out onto shore. As he sat there, dripping wet (and smelly!), thinking about what had happened, God spoke to him again. "Go to Nineveh, Jonah. Give them my message," he said.

And do you know what? This time Jonah was only too happy to do exactly as he was told! And the people of Nineveh heard God's message and were sorry, and God forgave them.

Reluctantly the sailors cast Jonah overboard. The second that he sank into the inky waters, the moment that he disappeared beneath the foamy crests of the waves, the storm ceased. It didn't die down. It just stopped. Instantly. And the sailors were filled with awe, and began to praise Jonah's God and to thank him for saving them.

As for Jonah, well, he sank slowly, inexorably down through the water. He had given himself into the hands of God, and was resigned to his fate, so it must have come as a bit of a shock when all of a sudden a huge shape appeared before him, and as he tried to focus, he made out a huge mouth with huge teeth! Before he knew it, he had been swallowed by an enormous fish! Swallowed whole!